Weekly Reader Book Club Presents

DRIVING ME CRAZY
Fun-on-Wheels Jokes

Compiled by Charles Keller
Illustrated by Lee Lorenz

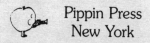

Pippin Press
New York

For Nicole and Leigh

This book is a presentation of Newfield Publications, Inc. Newfield Publications offers book clubs for children from preschool through high school. For further information write to: **Newfield Publications, Inc., 4343 Equity Drive, Columbus, Ohio 43228.**

Published by arrangement with Pippin Press. Newfield Publications is a federally registered trademark of Newfield Publications, Inc. Weekly Reader is a federally registered trademark of Weekly Reader Corporation.

Published by Pippin Press, 229 East 85th Street,
Gracie Station Box 1347, New York, N.Y. 10028

Printed in the United States of America
10 9 8 7 6 5 4 3 2

Library of Congress Cataloging-in-Publication Data

Keller, Charles.
    Driving me crazy: fun on wheels jokes / compiled by Charles
Keller: illustrated by Lee Lorenz.
    Summary: Jokes and riddles about cars, buses, trucks, bicycles,
motorcycles, and other vehicles on wheels. Example: What age is
important to a car? Mile-age.
    1. Motor vehicles—Juvenile humor. 2. Wheels — Juvenile humor.
3. Riddles, Juvenile. 4. Wit and humor, Juvenile. [1. Motor
vehicles—Wit and humor. 2. Vehicles—Wit and humor. 3. Wheels
—Wit and humor. 4. Jokes. 5. Riddles.] I. Lorenz, Lee, ill.
II. Title.
PN6231.M74K4 1989   88-39537
818'.5402—dc19
ISBN 0-945912-05-6:

How do you avoid being driven crazy?
Walk.

What is a banged-up car?
A car in first-crash condition.

How can you telephone from a car?
Who can't tell a phone from a car?

What was the turtle doing on the highway?
About a half-mile an hour.

What kind of cars do movie stars like?
Os-cars.

What do frogs give their cars when they won't start?
A jump start.

When is a car not a car?
When it turns into a driveway.

What's more remarkable than a robot that can walk?
A car that can run.

What do you call a large number of auto accidents?
A bumper crop.

What kind of truck does a ballerina drive?
A toe truck.

What do you get when you cross a donkey and a long-distance bus?
A travel burro.

What do you call a person who sells mobile homes?
A wheel-estate dealer.

What did the jack say to the car?
"Can I give you a lift?"

What did the policeman say after giving out a dozen tickets?
"I've done a fine day's work."

What kind of truck is always a "he"?
A mail truck.

What did the boy do with a dead battery?
He buried it.

What goes well with white walls?
Hubcaps.

What is a Laplander?
Someone who loses his balance on a bus.

What car makes the line down a road disappear?
A racer.

What happened to the snow tires the man bought for his car?
They melted.

Why did the traffic light turn red?
You would too if you had to change in the middle of the street.

How do they make anti-freeze?
They take away the blanket.

What was the vampire doing on the highway?
Looking for the main artery.

What did one windshield wiper say to the other?
"Isn't it a shame we only meet when it rains?"

Why did the police stop the man from making coffee in his car?
It was in a no perking zone.

What's green and rides in an ambulance?
A pear-medic.

How can you learn to drive fast?
Take a crash course.

Where is it okay to hit and run?
On a baseball field.

What did the Martian say to the gas pump?
"Take your finger out of your ear and listen to me!"

What gives milk and has a horn?
A milk truck.

Why did they open the first drive-in restaurant?
So people could curb their appetites.

What do you call a permit to ride a bike?
A peddler's license.

What's the difference between a car's back light and a short story?
One is a tail light and the other is a light tale.

What would you have if everyone in the country had a pink car?
A pink car nation.

What happened after the five-day bike race?
The racers got a weak end off.

What was the first bus to cross the ocean?
Columbus.

What kind of cars do frogs drive?
Hoprods.

Who rides around all day and tells people where to get off?
A bus driver.

What happened to the boy who thought he was a muffler?
He woke up exhausted.

What kind of shot do you give an automobile?
Fuel injection.

What kind of car do horses like?
An Oatsmobile.

What kind of skateboard breaks the first time you use it?
A cheap skate.

What do you call the life story of a car?
An autobiography.

Why did the man put his car in the oven?
He wanted a hot rod.

What kind of policemen enjoy their work best?
Traffic policemen, because they whistle while they work.

What goes on for miles and miles but never moves?
A highway.

What did one car say to the other after the accident?
"Haven't we bumped into each other before?"

What do you call a person who steals Japanese cars?
A Honda-taker.

What does an ape use to fix his car?
A monkey wrench.

What kind of car do rich rock stars drive?
A Rock-and-Rolls Royce.

What does a duck change a car's tires with?
A quacker jack.

What did one bicycle wheel say to the other?
"Was it you who spoke to me?"

What do you call a car for mice?
A Mouseratti.

What would you have if your car's engine started burning?
A fire engine.

What do you use when a wooden car has a flat tire?
A lumberjack.

Why did the man take his car out during the thunderstorm?
It was a driving rain.

What's harder than driving a car?
Paying for it.

What lives in the sea and carries a lot of people?
An octobus.

Why is an old car like a baby?
It never goes anywhere without a rattle.

Where do you eat on a highway?
Wherever there's a fork in the road.

What's gray, has two wheels and weighs four tons?
An elephant on a motorcycle.

What do you call a truck hauling a dozen-and-a-half pigs?
An 18-squealer.

What do you get when you cross a sports car with an egg?
Breakfast-to-go.

What ten letter word starts with gas?
Automobile.

What's big and yellow and comes in the morning to brighten mother's day?
The school bus.

What is the most dangerous part of a car?
The nut behind the wheel.

Why did the man use a spatula to fix his car?
Because the engine wouldn't turn over.

What kind of running means walking?
Running out of gas.

What did the man put on his car when it got cold?
An extra muffler.

What has two wheels, a horn and gives milk?
A cow on a motorcycle.

What did the farmer say when his pick-up skidded into the cornfield?
"Shucks."

What's black, wrinkled and makes pit stops?
A racing prune.

What happens to a boy who misses his bus and gets home late?
He catches it when he gets home.

What do you call a car packed in a crate?
A boxcar.

Why did the man look for the automobile in his garden?
He heard his car just came from the plant.

What do you call a tax on hitch hikers?
A thumb tax.

What's stranger than a Cadillac stretch?
A Mercedes Benz.

How do you get six elephants into a sports car?
Three in the front, two in the back and one in the glove compartment.

What do you call assistant used-car salesmen?
Lemon aides.

Why did the man take his fat uncle along on car trips?
Because his uncle had a spare tire.

Why couldn't the boy take the bus home?
His mother wouldn't let him keep it.

Where do old Volkswagens go?
To the old Volks home.

What do policemen put on peanut butter sandwiches?
Traffic jam.

What do you call elephants that ride on Greyhound buses?
Passengers.

What happens when tires get old?
They are retired.

Why did the man call his old car "Shasta"?
Shasta have new tires, shasta have a new battery and shasta have an oil change.

What's an underground parking garage?
A wall-to-wall car pit.

What sickness do racing drivers get?
Indygestion.

Why did the man sleep under an old car?
So he could get up oily in the morning.

What do you get when you cross two pizzas and a set of handle bars?
A piecycle.

Where do pigs park their cars?
At porking lots.

Who drives away all his customers?
A taxi-cab driver.

What's purple and goes "beep beep"?
A grape in a traffic jam.

What was the tow truck doing at the car race?
Trying to pull a fast one.

Why did the turtle cross the road?
To get to the Shell station.

What happens when you cross a bridge with a car?
You get to the other side.

How do you stop a dog from barking in the back seat of a car?
Have him sit in the front.

When do a car's brakes work best?
In the morning, because it's break-fast time.

How can you tell if a race car is sad?
When it's down in the pits.

How does an elephant get out of a sports car?
The same way he got in.

How much do used batteries cost?
Nothing. They're free of charge.

Why did the car get a flat tire?
There was a fork in the road.

FACE IT, BABY — THERE'S ELECTRICITY BETWEEN US.

What did the girl battery say to the boy battery?
"I get a charge out of you."

What driver doesn't have a license?
A screw driver.

What is the funniest car on the road?
A Jokeswagen.

What does a car hear with?
Its engine ears.

How do you get your car's motor to turn over?
Tickle it.

What age is important to a car?
Mile-age.

What equipment comes on a crying car?
Windshield weepers.